40 Day Devotions

Christopher Armour

40 *Daily Devotions* by Christopher Armour

 Published by Foxglove Press
1-877-205-1932
© 2004 Foxglove Press

All scriptures, except where noted, are from the Revised Standard Version.

ISBN 1-882959-55-8

Cover and text design by Barry Edwards, Armour&Armour
Editorial assistance by Linda Choate

First Edition 2005

40 Daily Devotions

To Granny,

who taught me to love those

most who deserve it least

Contents

Introduction

Learning God's will and understanding His purpose for us is not a Sunday-only enterprise but a full-time job. These devotions are intended to make you think every day—about yourself, and about your Lord.

Don't try to read this book from cover to cover. Instead, set aside a certain time of day for a brief study break. Think about the issues you have experienced or will confront tomorrow. Look in the mirror to see what you face, then choose a topic to help you reflect on God's will.

These forty lessons offer insights from sometimes surprising sources, words of inspiration to guide your thinking, and scriptures that demonstrate the word of God. Many topics include a daily prayer to help you put your feelings into your message to God.

I'd like to thank Erica Dailey, Phyllis Curtis, and most of all my wife Jan Stinson for helping me create these devotions for you.

—Christopher Armour

Happiness

Remember that happiness is a way
of travel, not a destination.

> Roy Goodman

Happiness always looks small
while you hold it in your hands,
but let it go, and you learn at
once how big and precious it is.

> Maxim Gorky

Be happy with what you have and
are, be generous with both, and you
won't have to hunt for happiness.

> William E. Gladstone

Happiness makes up in height
for what it lacks in length.

> Robert Frost

happiness

If you asked a dozen people, probably all of them would say they want to be happy. Everyone wants to be happy, right? In that case, how come so many people are unhappy?

The answer seems complicated at first. Some people think wealth, or power, or popularity will make them happy. They may spend huge amounts of energy for long periods of time pursuing the earthly reward they desire the most. Sadly, in many cases the happiness they expected still seems beyond their reach.

You can find the path to true happiness, if you look in the right place. All the guid-

Continued on next page

Behold, we call those happy who were steadfast. You have heard of the steadfastness of Job, and you have seen the purpose of the Lord, how the Lord is compassionate and merciful.
James 5:11

happiness

ance you need is found in God's word. Love God and keep His commandments; treat others as you want to be treated; do your best to walk in the footsteps of His Son. By following this path, you truly will find happiness.

He who gives heed to the word will prosper, and happy is he who trusts in the Lord.

Proverbs 16:20

My soul is bereft of peace, I have forgotten what happiness is; so I say, "Gone is my glory, and my expectation from the Lord."

Lamentations 3:17-18

And now, my sons, listen to me: happy are those who keep my ways.

Proverbs 8:32

O taste and see that the Lord is good! Happy is the man who takes refuge in him!

Psalm 34:8

40 Daily Devotions

happiness

*Dear Lord, thank You for
the rich blessings You bring
to me and my family every
day. Forgive me when I turn
my back on the bounty You
provide by looking for happiness in the ways of the world.
Guide me in Your Word,
and open my eyes to the
rewards You have given me,
for in them will I truly
be happy.*

Grief

Grief can't be shared. Everyone carries it alone, his own burdens, his own way.

Ann Morrow Lindbergh

Instead of weeping when a tragedy occurs in a songbird's life, it sings away its grief. I believe we could well follow the pattern of our feathered friends.

Robert S. Walker

Grief rends the heart cleanly, that it may begin to heal.

Morgan Llywelyn

grief

Just as funerals provide comfort for the living, grief is a symptom for survivors. It's the essence of loss, a reminder that we all share the same fate.

Although grief is an important part of the process of life and death, we can't let it overwhelm us. It can do serious physical and spiritual harm. There's a time to feel sorry for ourselves, but that time must come to an end.

We hurt. We heal. We move on.

When faced with death, we often fool ourselves about why we grieve. We think we feel sorry for the person who's gone. But aren't we really mourning for ourselves? After all, it's our loss, a new emptiness in our lives, our regret that our time together has ended.

Continued on next page

Even in laughter the heart is sad, and the end of joy is grief.
Proverbs 14:13

grief

In the early stages of grief, it's easy to reject God: anger, denial, and bargaining are negative emotions that raise barriers between us and our Savior. But when we finally arrive at the last stage, acceptance, we begin to learn the lessons of God, lessons we could not understand under other circumstances.

We accept God's message that life is short, that life is precious, that life is a gift. We emerge from our grief with stronger faith and greater joy in the promise of eternal life.

For the Lord will not cast off for ever, but, though he cause grief, he will have compassion according to the abundance of his steadfast love; for he does not willingly afflict or grieve the sons of men.

Lamentations 3:31-33

God himself will be with them; he will wipe away every tear from their eyes, and death shall be no more, neither shall there be mourning nor crying nor pain any more, for the former things have passed away.

Revelation 21:3-4

DAILY PRAYER

Dear Lord, even as my heart is filled with sorrow, I offer You thanks for the miracle of life and for the time You allowed me to spend with loved ones now departed. Please watch over me as I heal and comfort me with Your gentle touch. Forgive me for the pain I bring to others as I struggle with my own grief. Help me focus on the joy of living.

Compassion

Compassion is a two-way street.

Frank Capra

Everybody can be great
. . . because anybody can
serve. You don't have to have
a college degree to serve.
You don't have to make your
subject and verb agree
to serve. You only need a
heart full of grace. A soul
generated by love.

Martin Luther King Jr.

*Compassion is the only one of the human emotions the
Lord permitted Himself and it has carried the divine
flavor ever since.*

Dagobert Runes

compassion

When we see someone who is hurting, compassion should stir our hearts. We sympathize with their pain, and we may take a few minutes to commiserate with them.

Jesus had compassion for the crowds of people who flocked to see Him. He healed invalids, lepers, and people with disabilities of their physical infirmities, and He lifted up thousands who were suffering spiritually.

We can reflect Christ's compassion in our everyday lives, by looking beyond our own problems and passionately working to share and alleviate the pain of others.

The Lord is good to all, and his compassion is over all that he has made.

Psalm 145:9

As he went ashore he saw a great throng, and he had compassion on them, because they were like sheep without a shepherd; and he began to teach them many things.

Mark 6:34

Friendship

Be courteous to all, but intimate with few,
and let those few be well tried before you
give them your confidence. True friendship
is a plant of slow growth, and must undergo
and withstand the shocks of adversity
before it is entitled to the appellation.

George Washington

He who sows courtesy reaps
friendship, and he who plants
kindness gathers love.

Saint Basil

The glory of friendship is not the outstretched
hand, nor the kindly smile...it's the spiritual
inspiration that comes to one when he discovers
that someone else believes in him and is
willing to trust him with his friendship.

Ralph Waldo Emerson

friendship

You don't consider everyone that you know as a friend. Some can be described as associates and others as acquaintances. But when you think of your relationship with God, do you consider it a friendship?

Friendship is a relationship with a person whom you know, like, and trust. Is that how you would describe God? Do you know Him, like Him and trust Him? Think about how He would describe you. Would He say you are His friend, or an acquaintance?

Spend some time with God as you would with a friend. You then will realize that God offers the ultimate friendship.

Unfaithful creatures! Do you not know that friendship with the world is enmity with God? Therefore whoever wishes to be a friend of the world makes himself an enemy of God.

James 4:4

friendship

Lord, as I go through my life today, help me remember that You are my best friend and re-mind me to treat You that way. Let me not forget to talk to You or become too busy to consult You. Prevent me from speaking against You or ignoring Your will. And Lord, guide me to choose all my friends according to the standard You have shown me.

40 Daily Devotions

The Twenty-Third Psalm

The Lord is my shepherd, I shall not want;
he makes me lie down in green pastures.
He leads me beside still waters; he
restores my soul. He leads me in paths
of righteousness for his name's sake.

Even though I walk through the
valley of the shadow of death, I fear
no evil; for thou art with me; thy rod
and thy staff, they comfort me.

Thou preparest a table before me in the
presence of my enemies; thou anointest
my head with oil, my cup overflows.

Surely goodness and mercy shall follow
me all the days of my life; and I shall
dwell in the house of the Lord for ever.

Charity

I *expect to pass through life but once. If,
therefore, there can be any kindness I can
show, or any good things I can do to any fellow
human being, let me do it now, and not defer it
or neglect it, as I shall not pass this way again.*

William Penn

We make a living by what
we get, but we make a life
by what we give.

Winston Churchill

*The happiest people are those who care more
about others than they do about themselves.*

Ted Turner

charity

C harity means more than just writing a check. You realize the true benefits of charity only when you give of yourself without thought of reward.

As Christians, we send our love in two directions. First, of course, love flows to God our creator. This is a reflection of the Lord's total love for us, imperfect and unworthy as we are.

In turn, we extend this love to our less-fortunate neighbors. In this way we both show ourselves worthy of God's love and demonstrate that God's love is within us.

Remember that acts of charity are not performed for recognition. As Matthew says, "do not let your left hand know what your right hand is doing, so that your giving may be in secret." When you reach

Continued on next page

Each one must do as he has made up his mind, not reluctantly or under compulsion, for God loves a cheerful giver.
II Corinthians 9:7

charity

out to someone, the reward comes from within—and from above.

Those of us more fortunate have been blessed for a reason. We should thank God every day for the opportunities to do His work with our riches. Seek out those in need, and you will prosper all the more.

Do not lay up for yourselves treasures on earth, where moth and rust consume and where thieves break in and steal, but lay up for yourselves treasures in heaven, where neither moth nor rust consumes and where thieves do not break in and steal. For where your treasure is, there will your heart be also.

Matthew 6:19-21

Give, and it will be given to you; good measure, pressed down, shaken together, running over, will be put into your lap. For the measure you give will be the measure you get back.

Luke 6:38

charity

Dearest Father in Heaven, all my riches flow from You and all my blessings reflect Your goodness. I have nothing, except what You have given me. Therefore, help me, Father, to willingly and graciously share my bounty with those around me. Let me give without receiving credit and reach out without hope of recognition.

Redemption

*For as their Redeemer is mighty, and
is so exalted above all evil, so shall
they also be exalted in him.*

Jonathan Edwards

I know that suffering
awaits me. But to bear the
Redeemer's yoke is an
honor to one who has felt
the Redeemer's love.

John Geddie

*I admit I'm a lowly sinner. It's that admission
that led me to redemption and led me to Christ.*

George W. Bush

redemption

The book of John tells us that God sent His only begotten Son to earth to save us from sin. Jesus Christ is our Redeemer, our Savior who delivers us from the punishment of worldly despair.

Jesus takes us as worthless individuals who have no value save from the grace of God, and pays off our debts to let us enjoy free, godly lives. He exchanged His life on Earth for our eternal life in heaven. He redeemed us.

What price does He ask in return? Believe in the Lord, keep His commandments, and devote our lives to His good works.

In him we have redemption through his blood, the forgiveness of our trespasses, according to the riches of his grace.

Ephesians 1:7

O Israel, hope in the Lord! For with the Lord there is steadfast love, and with him is plenteous redemption.

Psalm 130:7

Humility

*Fullness of knowledge always means
some understanding of the depths
of our ignorance; and that is always
conducive to humility and reverence.*

Robert Millikan

What makes humility so
desirable is the marvelous
thing it does to us; it
creates in us a capacity
for the closest possible
intimacy with God.

Monica Baldwin

*Humility like darkness reveals
the heavenly lights.*

Henry David Thoreau

*It was pride that changed angels into devils;
it is humility that makes men as angels.*

Saint Augustine

humility

W̶e all know someone who could use a dose of humility, don't we? The ideal is that regardless of how high our station is in life, we must always treat others with dignity and respect.

The Lord Jesus is our perfect example of humility. He was "The King" yet he never raised himself above the people. He exemplified the qualities of modesty and respectfulness all the time. How inspirational that is for us!

When we believe that we have it all, that we know it all, remember Jesus and his walk on Earth.

Good and upright is the Lord; therefore he instructs sinners in the way. He leads the humble in what is right, and teaches the humble his way.

Psalm 25:8-9

humility

The reward for humility and fear of the LORD is riches and honor and life.

> Proverbs 22:4

Do nothing from selfishness or conceit, but in humility count others better than yourselves.

> Philippians 2:3

When you are invited by any one to a marriage feast, do not sit down in a place of honor, lest a more eminent man than you be invited by him; and he who invited you both will come and say to you, "Give place to this man," and then you will begin with shame to take the lowest place. But when you are invited, go and sit in the lowest place, so that when your host comes he may say to you, "Friend, go up higher"; then you will be honored in the presence of all who sit at table with you. For every one who exalts himself will be humbled, and he who humbles himself will be exalted.

> Luke 14:8-11

Toward the scorners he is scornful, but to the humble he shows favor.

> Proverbs 3:34

humility

My precious Father, thank
You for showing me favor
and supplying me with all of
these blessings. Help me
express my gratitude by
sharing my bounty with
others. Dear Lord, as I
share, remind me to remain
modest and not boastful,
respectful and not haughty,
humble and not inflated.

*C*ontentment

The secret of contentment is knowing how to
enjoy what you have, and to be able to lose
all desire for things beyond your reach.

Lin Yu-t'ang

As we become curators of
our own contentment . . .
we learn to savor the small
with a grateful heart.

Sarah Ban Breathnach

True contentment is a thing as active
as agriculture. It is the power of getting
out of any situation all that there is
in it. It is arduous and it is rare.

G.K. Chesterton

Sometimes when your life may be going exactly the way you want, you experience a positive feeling that you can't quite put your finger on. That feeling is contentment, a feeling that all is good in your spirit and God is watching and maintaining your well-being.

At that moment stop and smell the flowers, and savor the sweet taste of contentment. Then thank God for helping you find what you seek.

There is great gain in godliness with contentment; for we brought nothing into the world, and we cannot take anything out of the world;

I Timothy 6:6-7

For the sake of Christ, then, I am content with weaknesses, insults, hardships, persecutions, and calamities; for when I am weak, then I am strong.

II Corinthians 12:10

Keep your life free from love of money, and be content with what you have; for he has said, "I will never fail you nor forsake you."

Hebrews 13:5

Obedience

The purpose of problems
is to push you toward
obedience to God's laws,
which are exact and cannot
be changed. We have the free
will to obey them or disobey
them. Obedience will bring
harmony, disobedience will
bring you more problems.

Peace Pilgrim

One act of obedience is better
than one hundred sermons.

Dietrich Bonhoeffer

obedience

On a quiet day, when I ponder my purpose for being on this Earth, I marvel at God's mysterious plan. He created paradise as a place for us to live, yet He also gives us the power to abuse it. He gave us rules, laws, and commandments to follow, yet He gives us free will and infinite choice to disregard them.

Obedience comes easily sometimes, but not always. Sometimes we clearly know what the Lord has told us to do, and we choose not to do it. Many factors can keep us from obeying God's word, including fear of the reaction of others or lack of belief in our own strength. When you have trouble obeying God's will unconditionally, remember this. God never gives you an order that you don't have the ability to carry out successfully. Whatever He tells you to do, He gives you the strength to do it—and He has a divine reason for your instructions.

> But Peter and the apostles answered, "We must obey God rather than men."
>
> Acts 5:29

obedience

Dear Lord, help me today
to follow Your word and obey
Your will. Make me aware
of the obstacles that stand
in the way of my obedience,
and help me see the best
way around them. Please
forgive me when I falter.
Thank You for the rewards,
both material and spiritual,
that come from
my obedience.

The Beatitudes

Blessed are the poor in spirit, for
theirs is the kingdom of heaven.
Blessed are those who mourn, for
they shall be comforted.
Blessed are the meek, for they
shall inherit the earth.
Blessed are those who hunger and thirst for
righteousness, for they shall be satisfied.
Blessed are the merciful, for
they shall obtain mercy.
Blessed are the pure in heart,
for they shall see God.
Blessed are the peacemakers, for
they shall be called sons of God.
Blessed are those who are persecuted
for righteousness' sake, for theirs
is the kingdom of heaven.
Blessed are you when men revile you
and persecute you and utter all kinds of
evil against you falsely on my account.
Rejoice and be glad, for your reward is
great in heaven, for so men persecuted
the prophets who were before you.

Diligence

Against the backdrop of people who avoid work, cut corners, and do half-hearted jobs, a diligent man stands out. Practicing diligence is an excellent way to stand out for Christ at home, in the workplace, and even at church. Today, complete each one of your tasks, however big or small, with diligence.

Dr. David Jeremiah

Few things are impossible to diligence and skill. Great works are performed, not by strength, but perseverance.

Samuel Johnson

The expectations of life depend upon diligence; the mechanic that would perfect his work must first sharpen his tools.

Confucius

diligence

Working diligently is easy when we are doing something we like. In fact, sometimes we can get so absorbed in a labor of love that we don't even notice the passing of time.

Being diligent for the Lord involves more than just working hard. Giving our best effort is the foundation, but we also must pay steady attention to doing a good job and be heedful of every detail. We must have patience and commitment to see the work through to its end.

When we have finished the Lord's work, He will reward us for our diligence.

A *slack hand causes poverty, but the hand of the diligent makes rich.*

Proverbs 10:4

Thou hast commanded thy precepts to be kept diligently. O that my ways may be steadfast in keeping thy statutes!

Psalm 119:4-5

Thanksgiving

Thankfulness is the beginning of gratitude.
Gratitude is the completion of thankfulness.
Thankfulness may consist merely of
words. Gratitude is shown in acts.

Henri Frederic Amiel

Gratitude makes sense of
our past, brings peace for
today, and creates a vision
for tomorrow.

Melody Beattie

None is more impoverished than the
one who has no gratitude. Gratitude is a
currency that we can mint for ourselves,
and spend without fear of bankruptcy.

Fred De Witt Van Amburgh

thanksgiving

When you were a child, some loving adult probably taught you about the Magic Words: *please* and *thank you*. Now that you are adult, you understand the "magic" that comes from showing consideration and appreciation to others.

What about God? How often do you say please and thank you to Him? The Bible teaches us that we should "pray without ceasing." That's a far cry from saying a few words before meals and at bedtime.

Thanksgiving can be a state of mind. When you begin to think about it, the list of things to thank God for is virtually endless. You could start by naming the people you love most, listing the material blessings you enjoy every day, and celebrating the ability to

Continued on next page

I will praise the name of God with a song; I will magnify him with thanksgiving.

Psalm 69:30

do things that give you pleasure. If you wanted to devote an hour, or a full day, to enumerating reasons to be thankful, you still would only have scratched the surface.

Get in the habit of saying thank you to God. It's a great remedy for feeling discouraged, and it will remind you how many wonderful blessings you have.

O give thanks to the LORD, for he is good;
for his steadfast love endures for ever!
Let them thank the LORD for his steadfast love,
for his wonderful works to the sons of men!

Psalm 107:1, 8

Rejoice always, pray constantly, give thanks in all circumstances; for this is the will of God in Christ Jesus for you.

I Thessalonians 5:16-18

thanksgiving

Dear Heavenly Father,
Thank You for my family
and friends, for my good
health, and for a job that
lets me earn what I need in
life. Go with me today, and
open my eyes to sources of
joy that I may not have seen
before. In all things, help me
to give You credit for the joys
that come to me, for I know
I could do nothing alone.

Tolerance

In the practice of tolerance, one's
enemy is the best teacher.

Dalai Lama

No loss of flood and lightning,
no destruction of cities and
temples by hostile forces of
nature, has deprived man
of so many noble lives and
impulses as those which his
intolerance has destroyed.

Helen Keller

Tolerance is the eager and glad acceptance of
the way along which others seek the truth.

Sir Walter Besant

tolerance

L ife can throw some really unpleasant people our way. What can we do when they will not leave?

Well, look into their eyes so that you can see your own reflection. How can you not smile when you look at yourself? How can you not feel love when you look into your own eyes?

When we look closely at ourselves, it becomes easier to overlook annoying habits of others. Then we can embrace the aggravation they cause with love and tolerance.

Look into those eyes and smile because you know that you are a phenomenal person who can be tolerant of others.

And count the forbearance of our Lord as salvation.
II Peter 3:15

Courage

You gain strength, courage and confidence by every experience in which you really stop to look fear in the face. You are able to say to yourself, "I have lived through this horror. I can take the next thing that comes along." You must do the thing you think you cannot do.

Eleanor Roosevelt

courage

We often associate courage with famous figures and great deeds, but don't overlook the opportunities for bravery in your everyday life.

Speak out for what you believe. Stand up for those who can't defend themselves. Reach out for help when you can't make it alone. Set out to achieve your dreams.

These acts of courage bring rich rewards to those who can face—and overcome—their fears.

When Jesus called Peter out of the boat, His disciple walked upon the water—until he became frightened and began to

Continued on next page

> *For I know that through your prayers and the help of the Spirit of Jesus Christ this will turn out for my deliverance, as it is my eager expectation and hope that I shall not be at all ashamed, but that with full courage now as always Christ will be honored in my body, whether by life or by death.*
> Philippians 1:18-19

sink. Jesus caught him, saying, "You of little faith, why did you doubt?"

The foundation of courage is faith. Your belief in God's love will bring you the strength to do that which you think you cannot.

Be strong, and let your heart take courage, all you who wait for the LORD!

Psalms 31:24

Be watchful, stand firm in your faith, be courageous, be strong.

I Corinthians 16:13

But though we had already suffered and been shamefully treated at Philippi, as you know, we had courage in our God to declare to you the gospel of God in the face of great opposition.

I Thessalonians 2:2

courage

Father, forgive me when I forget Your power. I know with You behind me, I can accomplish anything, and I am thankful for that. Please give me courage to stand up for Your will. Let me not be frightened by challenges, but rather to embrace them with a certainty of victory because You are on my side.

Courage

Worry

Worry never robs tomorrow
of its sorrow, it only
saps today of its joy.

Leo Buscaglia

*I think that at some point in your life you
realize you don't have to worry if you do
everything you're supposed to do right.*

Joe Namath

*If our faith delivers us from worry, then
worry is an insult flung in the face of God.*

Robert Runcie

*Put your trust in the Lord and go
ahead. Worry gets you no place.*

Roy Acuff

I t's all too easy for anyone to fall into a "worry trap," focusing on anxieties and obsessing about problems until they take over our thoughts. Our worries feed on each other and we end up paralyzed, feeling helpless and alone.

These feelings are a sure sign that worrying goes against the will of God. Take a moment to think about the message such worrying sends. Aren't we demonstrating a lack of faith in His providence? Don't we show that we don't trust God to take care of us?

Matthew speaks of the lilies of the field. They do no work, they spin no clothing,

Continued on next page

And why are you anxious about clothing? Consider the lilies of the field, how they grow; they neither toil nor spin; yet I tell you, even Solomon in all his glory was not arrayed like one of these. But if God so clothes the grass of the field, which today is alive and tomorrow is thrown into the oven, will he not much more clothe you, O men of little faith?

Matthew 6:28-30

yet God blesses them with glorious raiments. We must believe that God provides for us, if He takes the time to care for more mundane creations.

We waste a lot of energy worrying, especially about things we cannot change. If you find yourself beset with anxieties over the future, try to turn your worries into prayer. Use God's guidance to make plans for tomorrow: Set goals, make schedules, and let tomorrow take care of itself.

Therefore do not worry about tomorrow, for tomorrow will worry about its own things. Sufficient for the day is its own trouble.

Matthew 6:34

Do not be anxious about anything, but in everything, by prayer and petition, with thanksgiving, present your requests to God. And the peace of God, which transcends all understanding, will guard your hearts and your minds in Christ Jesus.

Philippians 4:6-7

DAILY PRAYER

Father, thank You for managing my life. When the cares of the world pile up around me, help me to understand the destructiveness of worry. Remind me of the peace that comes from turning my cares over to You. Forgive me for trying to anticipate the future or fix things that I cannot change.

Atonement

The atonement was not the cause
but the effect of God's love.

Arthur Pink

People believe mistakenly,
that with death comes
atonement, when in reality,
life is for atonement and
Death is for Judgment.

Thomas A. Perez Sr.

40 Daily Devotions

atonement

A s Christians we are taught that we are born into sin. Does this exonerate us from living in the full power of God's presence? Of course not.

Even though it is inevitable that we will sin, when we do fall short we must repent. After we repent, we must atone for our sins.

The death of Jesus was the ultimate atonement for our sins, bringing reconciliation between God and the people. Jesus covers your sin. Atonement has already been made for you, and you are pure as snow.

For if, when we were enemies, we were reconciled to God by the death of his Son, much more, being reconciled, we shall be saved by his life. And not only so, but we also joy in God through our Lord Jesus Christ, by whom we have now received the atonement.

Romans 5:10-11 KJV

By loyalty and faithfulness iniquity is atoned for, and by the fear of the Lord a man avoids evil.

Proverbs 16:6

Conformity

Human progress is furthered, not by conformity, but by aberration.

H.L. Mencken

Success, recognition, and conformity are the bywords of the modern world where everyone seems to crave the anesthetizing security of being identified with the majority.

Martin Luther King Jr.

The race of man, while sheep in credulity, are wolves for conformity.

Carl Van Doren

We are half ruined by conformity, but we should be wholly ruined without it.

Charles Dudley Warner

40 Daily Devotions

conformity

P eer pressure can be brutal. It has the most impact on us when we are children and adolescents, but we never completely outgrow its reach. We always face the temptation to "go along with the crowd."

One of the major dangers of conformity comes directly from the devil. Satan uses our desire to conform to attack our own personal weak spot, whatever that might be. He knows we want others to accept us, and he uses our fear of not being accepted to convince us to take actions we know are wrong.

Celebrate your uniqueness, and appreciate the value of being one of a kind. And praise the Lord for giving you the free will to choose.

Do not be conformed to this world but be transformed by the renewal of your mind, that you may prove what is the will of God, what is good and acceptable and perfect.

Romans 12:2

conformity

Heavenly Father, help me today to take a stand for what I believe. Thank You for creating me exactly the way I am, and forgive me for wanting to be like everyone else. Give me courage to embrace my own uniqueness, and grant me strength to find my own way instead of going along with the crowd.

Parable: The Good Samaritan

Luke 10:30-37

A man was going down from Jerusalem to Jericho, and he fell among robbers, who stripped him and beat him, and departed, leaving him half dead.

Now by chance a priest was going down that road; and when he saw him he passed by on the other side. So likewise a Levite, when he came to the place and saw him, passed by on the other side.

But a Samaritan, as he journeyed, came to where he was; and when he saw him, he had compassion, and went to him and bound up his wounds, pouring on oil and wine; then he set him on his own beast and brought him to an inn, and took care of him. And the next day he took out two denarii and gave them to the innkeeper, saying, "Take care of him; and whatever more you spend, I will repay you when I come back."

Which of these three, do you think, proved neighbor to the man who fell among the robbers?

He said, "The one who showed mercy on him." And Jesus said to him, "Go and do likewise."

Love

*And in the end the love you take is
equal to the love you make.*

The Beatles

Hatred paralyzes life;
love releases it.

Hatred confuses life;
love harmonizes it.

Hatred darkens life;
love illumines it.

Martin Luther King Jr.

*Love does not consist in gazing at
each other, but in looking outward
together in the same direction.*

Antoine de Saint-Exupéry

love

L ove is the act of extending one-self for another's physical or spiritual well-being. Isn't it great when you can honestly say you love someone? Yet character is shown by the love he gives to someone we don't know, or better yet, to someone we do not want to love.

God's love is that way. He loves us even when we are not lovable. God does not withhold His love because we are not behaving by His principles. He gives His love freely and abundantly so we can see the true meaning of love—and find the right path.

Love should not be used to gratify ourselves but to lift up the broken spirit of all mankind. Without it, we are nothing.

We know that in everything God works for good with those who love him, who are called according to his purpose.
Romans 8:28

Love

love

If I speak in the tongues of men and of angels, but have not love, I am a noisy gong or a clanging cymbal. And if I have prophetic powers, and understand all mysteries and all knowledge, and if I have all faith, so as to remove mountains, but have not love, I am nothing.

If I give away all I have, and if I deliver my body to be burned, but have not love, I gain nothing.

Love is patient and kind; love is not jealous or boastful; it is not arrogant or rude. Love does not insist on its own way; it is not irritable or resentful; it does not rejoice at wrong, but rejoices in the right. Love bears all things, believes all things, hopes all things, endures all things. Love never ends; as for prophecies, they will pass away; as for tongues, they will cease; as for knowledge, it will pass away.

For our knowledge is imperfect and our prophecy is imperfect; but when the perfect comes, the imperfect will pass away.

When I was a child, I spoke like a child, I thought like a child, I reasoned like a child; when I became a man, I gave up childish ways. For now we see in a mirror dimly, but then face to face. Now I know in part; then I shall understand fully, even as I have been fully understood.

So faith, hope, love abide, these three; but the greatest of these is love.

1 Corinthians 13:1-13

love

Dear God in heaven, thank
You for the unconditional
love You have for me. Thank
You for lifting up my broken
spirit through Your grace.
Forgive me when I fail to
love others, especially those
I don't like. Help me to give
freely as You have given
to me.

Love

Generosity

*Logic and cold reason are poor weapons
to fight fear and distrust. Only faith
and generosity can overcome them.*

Jawaharlal Nehru

Generosity lies less in
giving much than in giving
at the right moment.

Jean De La Bruyère

*You will discover that you have two
hands. One is for helping yourself and
the other is for helping others.*

Audrey Hepburn

generosity

When I was a child, my mother taught me an important lesson: "The Lord loves a cheerful giver." Sharing with others, giving to good causes, spreading the Gospel—I believe we are directed by God to do these things. But my mother's lesson takes that one step further. Give, and be happy when you do it.

Everywhere you look, you see evidence of God's generosity. And most of us could list many people who have made our lives richer by generously giving to us. One way to show our appreciation for the gifts we receive is by cheerfully giving to others. We are blessed manyfold when we do.

You shall furnish him liberally out of your flock, out of your threshing floor, and out of your wine press; as the Lord your God has blessed you, you shall give to him.

Deuteronomy 15:14

generosity

Help me, dear Lord, to
appreciate the joy of giving,
even as You have richly
given to me. Thank You for
opening my eyes to
opportunities to share
my bounty, and forgive
me when I overlook the
blessing of sharing.

From Ecclesiastes

For everything there is a season, and a
time for every matter under heaven:
a time to be born, and a time to
die; a time to plant, and a time
to pluck up what is planted;
a time to kill, and a time to heal; a time
to break down, and a time to build up;
a time to weep, and a time to laugh; a
time to mourn, and a time to dance;
a time to cast away stones, and a time to
gather stones together; a time to embrace,
and a time to refrain from embracing;
a time to seek, and a time to lose; a
time to keep, and a time to cast away;
a time to rend, and a time to sew; a time
to keep silence, and a time to speak;
a time to love, and a time to hate; a
time for war, and a time for peace.

Mercy

All the great things are simple, and many
can be expressed in a single word: freedom,
justice, honor, duty, mercy, hope.

Winston Churchill

Our prayer and God's mercy
are like two buckets in a
well; while the one ascends
the other descends.

Mark Hopkins

I have always found that mercy bears
richer fruits than strict justice.

Abraham Lincoln

mercy

Mercy means showing compassion, even when the other person doesn't deserve it.

What's your first reaction when someone says something about you or does something to you that you think is unfair? If you are like most people, you experience a variety of negative feelings: resentment, anger, maybe an urge to get revenge.

God teaches us that the best thing to do when someone treats you unfairly is to show mercy to them, just like God is merciful to us when we do wrong. Showing mercy can be hard, especially when you can still feel the sting of being hurt. Yet, God always gives us a way to do His

Continued on next page

> But when the goodness and loving kindness of God our Savior appeared, he saved us, not because of deeds done by us in righteousness, but in virtue of his own mercy, by the washing of regeneration and renewal in the Holy Spirit.
>
> Titus 3:4-5

will. In His infinite wisdom, He has given us the strength to move beyond negative emotions and into the light of righteousness.

The answer is simple: Take your pain to God in prayer. Ask him to soften your heart and help you show kindness and mercy to the person who did wrong to you. Feel yourself surrounded by His love, and remember that our Heavenly Father opens His arms to all of us and shares his mercy with the world every day.

Have mercy on me, O God, according to thy steadfast love; according to thy abundant mercy blot out my transgressions.
Psalm 51:1

Blessed are the merciful, for they shall obtain mercy.
Matthew 5:7

Let us then with confidence draw near to the throne of grace, that we may receive mercy and find grace to help in time of need.

Hebrews 4:16

mercy

Dear Father, help me to understand Your grace and imitate Your mercy. Let me treat my enemies with compassion even when they don't deserve it, as You show compassionate love to me when I fall. Remind me every day that I have the blessing of salvation, in spite of my wrongdoings, because of You and Your merciful Son.

Mercy

Ambition

A man without ambition is
dead. A man with ambition
but no love is dead. A man
with ambition and love
for his blessings here on
earth is ever so alive.

Pearl Bailey

*A wise man is cured of ambition by ambition
itself; his aim is so exalted that riches, office,
fortune and favor cannot satisfy him.*

Samuel Johnson

Ambition is a dream with a V8 engine.

Elvis Presley

ambition

We all need ambition in order to maximize our potential. Ambition is a great tool to help us realize and accomplish our goals. It gives us a strong desire to achieve at a higher level, to strive to be better individuals.

The problem comes when we let ambition become a driving force in our lives. When that happens, we may lose sight of focusing on worthy goals. Without proper governance, ambition can lead us to other ungodly characteristics like greed, selfishness, or arrogance.

Put your ambition in God's hands, and ask Him to shape your ambitious energy to His glory.

For where jealousy and selfish ambition exist, there will be disorder and every vile practice.

James 3:16

Anger

*Anger is a wind which blows out
the lamp of the mind.*

Robert Ingersoll

Holding on to anger is like
grasping a hot coal with
the intent of throwing it
at someone else; you are
the one getting burned.

Buddha

40 Daily Devotions

anger

Frustration, insecurity, loss, injustice, helplessness, criticism, resentment, thoughtlessness . . . the causes of our anger are legion and the results are inevitable. Everybody gets angry sometimes, and we can't expect others (or ourselves) not to get mad. After all, even Jesus lost his temper!

It's how we act upon our anger that's important. We must avoid the destructive power anger raises within us. We usually react by lashing out or holding in— the one way hurts others and the second hurts you.

The best way to deal with your anger is by breaking it into stages. First, recognize your anger. Learn how it makes you act so you can diagnose the next incident.

Continued on next page

> *Everyone should be quick to listen, slow to speak and slow to become angry, for man's anger does not bring about the righteous life that God desires.*
>
> James 1:19-20

anger

When you realize that you're angry, identify the source. Is it external (someone has done or said something) or internal (you're not happy with how you've behaved)?

The next step is to address your anger appropriately. Don't blow up in public or sulk in your room; find the right time and place for the most important step.

Express your anger simply and directly. If you're having trouble putting your feelings into words, try drawing a picture of your anger to help you focus.

Finally, remember that anger creates obligations. You have an obligation to yourself to express your anger. You have an obligation to those that upset you to share your anger. And you have an obligation to God to overcome your anger so you can lead a righteous life.

anger

O Lord, thank You for giving me the power to control my anger. I know that You have provided a way for me to learn from unpleasant experiences, and when I succumb to anger I am unable to learn. Forgive me for lashing out at others or holding my anger inside. Help me to overcome my anger so that I may better serve You.

Hypocrisy

As witnesses not of our intentions but of our conduct, we can be true or false, and the hypocrite's crime is that he bears false witness against himself. What makes it so plausible to assume that hypocrisy is the vice of vices is that integrity can indeed exist under the cover of all other vices except this one. Only crime and the criminal, it is true, confront us with the perplexity of radical evil; but only the hypocrite is really rotten to the core.

Hannah Arendt

Hypocrisy, the lie, is the true sister of evil, intolerance, and cruelty.

Raisa M. Gorbachev

40 Daily Devotions

hypocrisy

W e've all met them: people who say one thing to your face, and something entirely different behind your back. You might call them two-faced, hypocritical, or insincere. The one thing you probably do not want to call them is "friend."

Jesus deplored the actions of hypocrites during his lifetime, and he cautioned His disciples about them. He warned that people who make a big show of praying or who seek acclaim for doing good deeds are not earning the Father's favor. Rather, they have already received their "reward": the praise of men.

Search your heart every day to make sure

Continued on next page

Why do you see the speck that is in your brother's eye, but do not notice the log that is in your own eye? Or how can you say to your brother, "Let me take the speck out of your eye," when there is the log in your own eye? You hypocrite, first take the log out of your own eye, and then you will see clearly to take the speck out of your brother's eye.

Matthew 7:3-5

your actions come from God's word. Do
the right thing because He commands it,
not because you want human praise. Take
every step as though God is looking over
your shoulder—because He is.

*So you also outwardly appear righteous to men, but within
you are full of hypocrisy and iniquity.*

Matthew 23:28

*And when you pray, you must not be like the hypocrites; for
they love to stand and pray in the synagogues and at the
street corners, that they may be seen by men. Truly, I say to
you, they have received their reward.*

Matthew 5:5

*Thus, when you give alms, sound no trumpet before you, as
the hypocrites do in the synagogues and in the streets, that
they may be praised by men. Truly, I say to you, they have
received their reward.*

Matthew 6:2

hypocrisy

God, keep me walking in
the way You guide. Let my
actions glorify You and my
words praise Your wisdom.
Forgive me when I talk in a
harmful way about others,
and remind me that my
failings leave me undeserving
of Your grace. Help me to
treat others as I want to
be treated.

Trust

Anxiety in human life is what squeaking
and grinding are in machinery that
is not oiled. In life, trust is the oil.

Henry Ward Beecher

Doubt and mistrust are the mere panic of timid
imagination, which the steadfast heart will
conquer, and the large mind will transcend.

Helen Keller

All I have seen teaches
me to trust the Creator
for all I have not seen.

Ralph Waldo Emerson

I am sustained by a sense of the
worthwhileness of what I am doing; a trust
in the good faith of the process which created
and sustains me. That process I call God.

Upton Sinclair

trust

One of the greatest blessings of being God's child is that we can trust Him to lead us along the right path for our lives. When we put our unquestioning trust in God, we can be confident that every day is unfolding exactly as it should. That's easy to do when life is going well, but harder to do in difficult times.

When you feel doubts about your actions or get worried about what the future holds, take your troubles to God in prayer. Jesus taught us the importance of placing complete trust in God; he died on the cross because it was God's will, and he taught us in the Lord's Prayer that we must put God's kingdom and God's will ahead of our own.

The Lord is my strength and my shield; in him my heart trusts; so I am helped, and my heart exults, and with my song I give thanks to him.   Psalm 28:7

Pray then like this: Our Father who art in heaven, Hallowed be thy name. Thy kingdom come. Thy will be done, On earth as it is in heaven.   Matthew 6: 9-10

Trust

trust

O Lord, help me to walk
the way You want me to go.
Help me to trust in Your
power and absolute good-
ness. Let me not worry
about earthly concerns, but
rather put myself completely
in Your hands. You know
what is best for me, and
I willingly give myself to
Your guidance.

Parable: The Maidens and the Lamps

Matthew 25:1-13

The kingdom of heaven shall be compared to ten maidens who took their lamps and went to meet the bridegroom.

Five of them were foolish, and five were wise. For when the foolish took their lamps, they took no oil with them; but the wise took flasks of oil with their lamps.

As the bridegroom was delayed, they all slumbered and slept. But at midnight there was a cry, "Behold, the bridegroom! Come out to meet him." Then all those maidens rose and trimmed their lamps. And the foolish said to the wise, "Give us some of your oil, for our lamps are going out." But the wise replied. "Perhaps there will not be enough for us and for you; go rather to the dealers and buy for yourselves."

And while they went to buy, the bridegroom came, and those who were ready went in with him to the marriage feast; and the door was shut. Afterward the other maidens came also, saying, "Lord, lord, open to us." But he replied, "Truly, I say to you, I do not know you."

Watch therefore, for you know neither the day nor the hour.

Integrity

A single lie destroys a whole
reputation of integrity.

Baltasar Gracian

Subtlety may deceive you; integrity never will.

Oliver Cromwell

To give real service you must
add something which cannot
be bought or measured
with money, and that is
sincerity and integrity.

Douglas Adams

The glue that holds all relationships
together—including the relationship
between the leader and the led—is
trust, and trust is based on integrity.

Brian Tracy

integrity

Y ou may be fortunate enough to have a friend who is steady as a rock. That person is firm in their moral beliefs and does not waiver under any circumstances. When they say *yes* they mean *yes*, and when they say *no* they mean *no*—regardless of the stakes.

Are you one of those people? Do you have the integrity to stand by your moral beliefs in spite of what others may think?

God wants you to be that steadfast person who does not waiver. He wants you to be just like He is, steady as a rock.

The wicked is overthrown through his evil-doing, but the righteous finds refuge through his integrity.

Proverbs 14:32

Show yourself in all respects a model of good deeds, and in your teaching show integrity, gravity, and sound speech that cannot be censured, so that an opponent may be put to shame, having nothing evil to say of us.

Titus 2:7-8

Temptation

Remember not only to say the right thing in the right place, but far more difficult still, to leave unsaid the wrong thing at the tempting moment.

Benjamin Franklin

Temptation is giving in when you should be holding out.

Joseph Martino

Evil indulged in eventually becomes evil that controls us.

John White

Saintliness is also a temptation.

Jean Anouilh

Tis one thing to be tempted, another thing to fall.

William Shakespeare

temptation

Children learn at an early age the basic difference between right and wrong. Sharing with others is right; hitting is wrong. Saying "thank you" is right; cursing is wrong.

As adults, the issues get more complicated and the line of distinction becomes less clear. We receive conflicting messages about right and wrong, and we may see people we like and respect doing things we know in our heart is wrong. They may even encourage us to join them in inappropriate actions.

We face temptations every day because God wants us to know sin and understand its effects on our lives.

Continued on next page

> No temptation has overtaken you that is not common to man. God is faithful, and he will not let you be tempted beyond your strength, but with the temptation will also provide the way of escape, that you may be able to endure it.
> I Corinthians 10:13

temptation

God always listens when we ask for his help. Go to God in prayer, and tell him about the situation you are facing. Ask him to help you see the right path to follow—and then listen for his answer. It will guide you to peace and joy.

Watch and pray that you may not enter into temptation; the spirit indeed is willing, but the flesh is weak."

Matthew 26:41

No temptation has overtaken you that is not common to man. God is faithful, and he will not let you be tempted beyond your strength, but with the temptation will also provide the way of escape, that you may be able to endure it.

I Corinthians 10:13

It is like sport to a fool to do wrong, but wise conduct is pleasure to a man of understanding.

Proverbs 10:23

temptation

O, Lord, I understand
the difference in right and
wrong, and yet I am tempted
to do wrong. Please give me
the strength to trust in Your
will, and to place my faith
in Your law. Help me when
I am weak to follow Your
Word, for I know Your
blessings will come to me.

Temptation

Greed

Form no covetous desire, so that the demon of greediness may not deceive thee, and the treasure of the world may not be tasteless to thee.

Zoroaster

From top to bottom of the ladder, greed is aroused without knowing where to find ultimate foothold. Nothing can calm it, since its goal is far beyond all it can attain.

Emile Durkheim

There is a very fine line between loving life and being greedy for it.

Maya Angelou

There is sufficiency in the world for man's need but not for man's greed.

Mahatma Gandhi

greed

Greed is one of the devil's favorite tools. "You would be happier if you had more. . . ." More money, more jewels, more possessions, more everything. Of course, the Bible teaches us that just the opposite is true. Only when we turn our backs on greed will we receive true riches. As the saying goes, money doesn't buy happiness.

Often greed motivates us to make decisions and take actions that are against God's will. And greed is the epitome of failing to appreciate the blessings we have been given by God. Practice turning your back to greed by making an extra effort to share your bounty with others. When you catch yourself wanting more, more, more, ask yourself how much happier you could be with less, less, less.

A *greedy man stirs up strife, but he who trusts in the Lord will be enriched.*

Proverbs 28:25

Greed

greed

God, forgive me when I am greedy. Help me to see that You have provided everything I need, and lead me to share more freely when I feel most greedy. Thank You for taking care of me, and please continue to bless me richly, as You have already.

The Lord's Prayer

Matthew 6:9-15 KJV

After this manner therefore pray ye: Our Father
which art in heaven, Hallowed be thy name.
Thy kingdom come. Thy will be done
in earth, as it is in heaven.
Give us this day our daily bread.
And forgive us our debts, as
we forgive our debtors.
And lead us not into temptation, but deliver
us from evil: For thine is the kingdom, and
the power, and the glory, for ever. Amen.
For if ye forgive men their trespasses, your
heavenly Father will also forgive you:
But if ye forgive not men their trespasses,
neither will your Father forgive your trespasses.

Truth

A dog barks when his master is attacked. I would be a coward if I saw that God's truth is attacked and yet would remain silent.

John Calvin

A few observations and much reasoning lead to error; many observations and a little reasoning lead to truth.

Alexis Carrel

You cannot be truthful if you are not courageous.

Osho

When I despair, I remember that all through history the way of truth and love have always won.

Mahatma Gandhi

truth

These days, some people would have us believe that truth is relative, something that changes from one circumstance to the next—as though that makes it okay for us to be untruthful.

But there is only one truth and that is God's truth. God's truth is so full of honesty, sincerity, and integrity that you recognize it immediately; so much so, that it is the truth that does not have to be stated.

Living and walking in truth is the greatest path to the righteous of the Lord. Our example of divine truth is the walk of Jesus. Jesus was faithful to the truth of God and steadfast in His beliefs. This is what God expects from us as well.

Lead me in thy truth, and teach me, for thou art the God of my salvation; for thee I wait all the day long.

Psalm 25:5

Truth

Forgiveness

Forgiveness does not change the past,
but it does enlarge the future.

Paul Boese

Forgiveness unleashes joy. It brings peace.
It washes the slate clean. It sets all the
highest values of love in motion. In a sense,
forgiveness is Christianity at its highest level.

John MacArthur

Forgiveness is not an
occasional act; it is a
permanent attitude.

Martin Luther King Jr.

The glory of Christianity is to
conquer by forgiveness.

William Blake

forgiveness

Forgiveness should be one of the easiest of God's lessons to learn. After all, we live in a constant state of forgiveness—we are all sinners, yet God forgives us time and again.

But all too often this lesson is lost on us: We nurse our grievances in our breast, we refuse to relinquish blame, we remember wrongs long after the hurt is gone.

That's because it requires great strength to forgive—like the strength Jesus Christ showed as he suffered on the cross yet asked his Father to forgive us. It's easy to hold a grudge and very difficult to let go of bitterness and pain.

But the act of forgiveness is the beginning of healing. When we forgive, we're able to

Continued on next page

For if you forgive men their trespasses, your heavenly Father also will forgive you; but if you do not forgive men their trespasses, neither will your Father forgive your trespasses.
Matthew 6:14-15

look past the mistake someone has made to see the truth in their hearts. This frees us from our pain and brings us peace. And it shows them that we love them despite their actions.

Peter asked Jesus how often we must forgive. Not seven times, Christ said, but "seventy times seven." Forgive people until you lose count, he says, and it stops being an attitude and becomes a state of being.

Let us lay down the burden of our anger and shrug off our hurts by living a life of forgiveness. Don't "forgive and forget." Forgive and move forward in peace and love.

You have heard that it was said, "An eye for an eye and a tooth for a tooth." But I say to you, Do not resist one who is evil. But if any one strikes you on the right cheek, turn to him the other also.

Matthew 5:38-39

forgiveness

Lord, I know I am in need of Your forgiveness every day, and yet sometimes I am reluctant to forgive others. Please help me to graciously forgive the hurts and injustices of those around me. Let me find peace in Your perfect love, and guide me to extend forgiveness generously, especially to those who do not ask for it.

Forgiveness

Hope

*Ah, Hope! What would life be, stripped of
thy encouraging smiles, that teach us to
look behind the dark clouds of to-day, for the
golden beams that are to gild the morrow.*

Susanna Moodie

Hope is the thing
with feathers—

That perches in the soul—

And sings the tunes
without the words—

And never stops—at all—.

Emily Dickinson

*All human wisdom is summed up
in two words—wait and hope.*

Alexandre Dumas, pére

hope

Whenever we have a bad day, there's always one thing that can keep us going: hope.

Hope is more than a wish or dream. Hope encompasses the belief that what we wish for or dream of can actually be attained. We wish we could win a million dollars; we hope we can manage our money wisely enough to be financially secure.

God offers us hope in the midst of earthly despair. When Abraham was distraught at not having children, God told him not to give up hope. He promised that Abraham's offspring would eventually populate the world—and He fulfilled that promise. Through faith in God, we can always have hope for better days.

Why are you cast down, O my soul, and why are you disquieted within me? Hope in God; for I shall again praise him, my help and my God.

Psalm 42:5-6

hope

Lord, lift me up when life leaves me in despair. Thank You for giving me hope, because I know You fulfill Your promises and will make everything work for my good. Forgive me when I close my eyes to the rewards You have waiting for me.

40 Daily Devotions

Parable: The Wise Man Builds His House upon the Rock
Matthew 7:24-29

"Every one then who hears these words of mine and does them will be like a wise man who built his house upon the rock;

and the rain fell, and the floods came, and the winds blew and beat upon that house, but it did not fall, because it had been founded on the rock.

And every one who hears these words of mine and does not do them will be like a foolish man who built his house upon the sand;

and the rain fell, and the floods came, and the winds blew and beat against that house, and it fell; and great was the fall of it."

And when Jesus finished these sayings, the crowds were astonished at his teaching,

Mistakes

I seem to have made more mistakes than any others of whom I know, but have learned thereby to make ever swifter acknowledgment of the errors and thereafter immediately set about to deal more effectively with the truths disclosed by the acknowledgment of erroneous assumptions.

Richard Buckminster Fuller

Even the knowledge of
my own fallibility cannot
keep me from making
mistakes. Only when I
fall do I get up again.

Vincent Van Gogh

A life spent making mistakes is not only more honorable but more useful than a life spent doing nothing.

George Bernard Shaw

mistakes

No one on Earth is perfect, and everyone makes mistakes from time to time. That's a part of being human. The good side of making mistakes is that every mistake offers us an opportunity to learn. And every time we learn, we add to our wisdom.

The most important lesson to learn from a mistake is what went wrong. When we understand how the mistake happened, we can avoid it in the future.

Another benefit that comes from making mistakes is learning how to behave with honor and set things right. First, we must apologize to the people who've been hurt by our mistake. Then, we must do what we can to clean up the mess we made—take responsibility for our ac-

Continued on next page

Just so, I tell you, there will be more joy in heaven over one sinner who repents than over ninety-nine righteous persons who need no repentance.

Luke 15:7

Mistakes

mistakes

tions and minimize the pain it brings to others.

Our Heavenly Father knows and understands about mistakes. He's always ready to forgive us and turn a mistake into something for our good and for His glory. Rejoice in this knowledge, and freely forgive yourself as well.

The fear of the Lord is the beginning of knowledge; fools despise wisdom and instruction.

Proverbs 1:7

Repent therefore, and turn again, that your sins may be blotted out, that times of refreshing may come from the presence of the Lord.

Acts 3:19

But the wisdom from above is first pure, then peaceable, gentle, open to reason, full of mercy and good fruits, without uncertainty or insincerity.

James 3:17

mistakes

Dear Father, I know I
make mistakes, and
for that I apologize.
Thank You for forgiving
me and helping me to
learn from my mistakes.
Guide me according to
Your word, that I gain
wisdom and follow
Your will.

Mistakes

Faith

By faithfulness we are collected and wound
up into unity within ourselves, whereas we
had been scattered abroad in multiplicity.

Saint Augustine

Every tomorrow has two handles. We can take
hold of it with the handle of anxiety or the
handle of faith. We should live for the future,
and yet find our life in the fidelities of the
present; the last is only the method of the first.

Henry Ward Beecher

Faith is building on what you know is here, so you can reach what you know is there.

Cullen Hightower

Faith is like radar that sees through the
fog—the reality of things at a distance
that the human eye cannot see.

Corrie Ten Boom

40 Daily Devotions

faith

As we walk through our daily lives, sometimes we face challenges that may seem to be too much for us to handle. And yet, because we trust the wisdom of God, we know we have the strength to overcome obstacles. That's where faith comes in.

We have faith because we believe with absolute certainty in the trustworthiness of God. Throughout the Bible, we find examples of His convincing dependability. He delivered the Israelites from Egyptian bondage, saved Noah and his family from the great flood, protected Daniel from the lions. When Jesus performed miracles during His life on Earth, He reminded the crowds of the power of faith: healing the sick, raising Lazarus from the dead, allowing Peter to walk on water. And through

Continued on next page

Know therefore that the Lord your God is God, the faithful God who keeps covenant and steadfast love with those who love him and keep his commandments, to a thousand generations.
Deuteronomy 7:9

Faith

His Son Jesus Christ, God promises that those who are faithful to Him will rejoice with Him throughout eternity.

Yet, even with so many reasons to have absolute faith in God, everyone has weak moments when we feel abandoned or discouraged. We let mundane matters bother us and stumble under the burden of worry.

Those are the times that our faith can be most valuable to us. Placing your faith in God can be a great stress reliever. Leave the worry to Him; He knows how to lead you to a place of peace. If you have trouble surrendering your cares to the Lord, try this: Picture yourself gathering up everything that worries you, and stuffing it inside a big balloon. Now mentally release the balloon and watch it float toward the heavens, into the hands of God. When the balloon has floated out of sight, you can rest easy, knowing that God has your cares completely under control.

faith

Dear God, I know You have absolute power over Heaven and Earth. I know that You have control over situations that I do not understand. Father, help me have faith in Your divine wisdom and to place myself in Your hands. Forgive me when my faith is shaken, and lift me up when I fall.

Faith

Adversity

In every adversity there lies the seed
of an equivalent advantage. In every
defeat is a lesson showing you how
to win the victory next time.

Robert Collier

Comfort and prosperity have never enriched the world as much as adversity has.

Billy Graham

One who gains strength by overcoming
obstacles possesses the only strength
which can overcome adversity.

Albert Schweitzer

You don't develop courage by being
happy in your relationships every day.
You develop it by surviving difficult
times and challenging adversity.

Barbara De Angelis

40 Daily Devotions

adversity

You can't journey through life without facing adversity. None of us knows its nature—death, illness, betrayal, or failure—but we can count on its arrival, usually at the time we're worst prepared for it.

How we face our troubles reveals the shape of our character and the strength of our faith. We can fall before the buffets of bad fortune, or we can bow our backs and triumph with the help of our faith.

Adversity comes into our lives for many reasons. You may be facing a test of your character. It may arise as a temptation to sin. Or it may be God's way of teaching you the way.

Continued on next page

I have said this to you, that in me you may have peace. In the world you have tribulation; but be of good cheer, I have overcome the world.

John 16:33

adversity

The Apostle Paul suffered terribly but never gave up. "I am well content with weaknesses, with insults, with distresses, with persecutions, with difficulties, for Christ's sake," he said, "for when I am weak, then I am strong."

Adversity puts our relationship with God into perspective. We gain strength as we realize our weaknesses. And we build our faith when we recognize our fears.

In the day of prosperity be joyful, and in the day of adversity consider; God has made the one as well as the other, so that man may not find out anything that will be after him.
Ecclesiastes 7:14

And though the Lord give you the bread of adversity and the water of affliction, yet your Teacher will not hide himself any more, but your eyes shall see your Teacher. And your ears shall hear a word behind you, saying, "This is the way, walk in it," when you turn to the right or when you turn to the left.
Isaiah 30:20-21

adversity

Heavenly Father, thank You
for making me strong. Help
me to face adversities secure
in the knowledge that You
are with me. Let me face
troubled times armed with
the power of my faith and
Your love. Forgive me when
I fail to see the blessings that
lie inside misfortunes.

Adversity

Guilt

Every man is guilty of all the good he didn't do.

Voltaire

The guilty one is not he who commits the
sin, but the one who causes the darkness.

Victor Hugo

Each snowflake in an avalanche pleads not guilty.

Stanislaw J. Lem

From the body of one guilty deed a thousand
ghostly fears and haunting thoughts proceed.

William Wordsworth

Guilt: the gift that keeps on giving.

Erma Bombeck

Guilt is not a feeling that God bestows on His believers. Rather, Satan uses guilt to make us hide our face and turn away from God.

When you feel that you have done something so wrong that God will not have compassion for you, remember the principle of forgiveness. God will always forgive and grant mercy to those who ask for it. So ask for His mercy, and release yourself from the burden of guilt.

I will cleanse them from all the guilt of their sin against me, and I will forgive all the guilt of their sin and rebellion against me.

Jeremiah 33:8

The way of the guilty is crooked, but the conduct of the pure is right.

Proverbs 21:8

Guilt

Vanity

Vanity is the quicksand of reason.

George Sand

Cure yourself of the affliction
of caring how you appear
to others. Concern yourself
only with how you appear
before God, concern yourself
only with the idea that
God may have of you.

Miguel De Unamuno

Pride that dines on vanity, sups on contempt.

Benjamin Franklin

*There is nothing so agonizing to the fine skin
of vanity as the application of a rough truth.*

Edward G. Bulwer-Lytton

40 Daily Devotions

vanity

None of us has any reason to be vain, yet sometimes we are. We falsely believe that in some way our own worth exceeds the grace of God.

Sometimes we cross the line from being proud of our accomplishments to being arrogant. We take too much of the credit ourselves, instead of attributing it to God. We get puffed up about our own (perceived) superiority.

Whatever we achieve, all of the glory belongs to God. He made us as we are, in His image.

If any one thinks he is religious, and does not bridle his tongue but deceives his heart, this man's religion is vain.

James 1:26

For all that is in the world, the lust of the flesh and the lust of the eyes and the pride of life, is not of the Father but is of the world.

I John 2:16

What is your life? For you are a mist that appears for a little time and then vanishes. Instead you ought to say, "If the Lord wills, we shall live and we shall do this or that." As it is, you boast in your arrogance. All such boasting is evil.

James 4:14-16

When pride comes, then comes disgrace; but with the humble is wisdom.

Proverbs 11:2

A man's pride will bring him low, but he who is lowly in spirit will obtain honor.

Proverbs 29:23

Charm is deceitful, and beauty is vain, but a woman who fears the Lord is to be praised.

Proverbs 31:30

Talk no more so very proudly, let not arrogance come from your mouth; for the Lord is a God of knowledge, and by him actions are weighed.

I Samuel 2:3

vanity

Heavenly Father, thank
You for making me in Your
divine image. Forgive me
when I put my faith in
myself instead of in You.
Help me to see my own
achievements and goodness
as a reflection of Your glory.

Fear

Action conquers fear.

Peter Nivio Zarlenga

As the ostrich when
pursued hideth his head,
but forgetteth his body;
so the fears of a coward
expose him to danger.

Akhenaton

Commit yourself to a dream. Nobody who tries
to do something great but fails is a total failure.
Why? Because he can always rest assured
that he succeeded in life's most important
battle—he defeated his fear of trying.

Robert Schuller

Do the thing you fear and the
death of fear is certain.

Ralph Waldo Emerson

fear

Fear is a natural human emotion, an important signal to protect us from harm. But fear also can be harmful and destructive when it keeps us from witnessing for the Lord.

Jesus once told his apostles that if they had as much faith as a grain of mustard seed, they would be able to move a mountain from one place to another. With a promise like that, who knows what earthly obstacles we can overcome when we reject fear?

God has promised us that He will save us when we let Him be in charge. He will take us where we should go; He will protect us from our enemies; He will meet our needs forever. We can be fearless because we are safe in the arms of God.

Hence we can confidently say, "The Lord is my helper, I will not be afraid; what can man do to me?"

Hebrews 13:6

Fear

fear

Fear not, little flock, for it is your Father's good pleasure to give you the kingdom.

Luke 12:32

Be not afraid of them, for I am with you to deliver you, says the Lord.

Jeremiah 1:8

The Lord is my light and my salvation; whom shall I fear? The Lord is the stronghold of my life; of whom shall I be afraid?

Psalm 27:1

A storm of wind came down on the lake, and they were filling with water, and were in danger. And they went and woke him, saying, "Master, Master, we are perishing!" And he awoke and rebuked the wind and the raging waves; and they ceased, and there was a calm. He said to them, "Where is your faith?" And they were afraid, and they marveled, saying to one another, "Who then is this, that he commands even wind and water, and they obey him?"

Luke 8:23-25

fear

Oh, Lord, forgive me when fear holds me back and shakes my faith in You. Pick me up when I stumble, and point my feet in the right direction. Help me turn myself over to You and look to You when I am afraid, because I know You will protect me from harm.

Fear

Mournfulness

Sadness does not inhere in things; it does not reach us from the world and through mere contemplation of the world. It is a product of our own thought. We create it out of whole cloth.

Emile Durkheim

The walls we build around us to keep sadness out also keep out the joy.

Jim Rohn

mournfulness

It is so easy to get stuck in the past: remembering the lost loves, the lost jobs, the forgotten dreams.

Living in the past causes us to long for things that are gone, thereby giving us a heavy heart. We experience sadness on a daily basis. But the past is the past; it is gone; accept it and move on. Enjoy today like it is the best day of your life. Paint your face with a smile, and allow your heart to be light.

Experience the feeling of letting go of old sorrows. Embrace the present with all that you have and move beyond the past. Your reward comes from joy in the Lord.

Thou hast turned for me my mourning into dancing; thou hast loosed my sackcloth and girded me with gladness.

Psalm 30:11

I will turn their mourning into joy, I will comfort them, and give them gladness for sorrow.

Jeremiah 31:13

Patience

He that can have patience
can have what he will.

Benjamin Franklin

Our real blessings often
appear to us in the shape
of pains, losses and
disappointments; but let
us have patience and we
soon shall see them in
their proper figures.

Joseph Addison

Never think that God's delays are
God's denials. Hold on; hold fast;
hold out. Patience is genius.

George-Louis Leclerc de Buffon

patience

Everything, all at once, right now! In today's fast-paced world, we sometimes overlook the importance of being patient. Having been raised in an instant-gratification society, we may unconsciously slip into the right-this-minute mentality. Sadly, we miss many of the joys the Lord makes available to us when we get in a hurry.

When the sun rises, the motion is subtle. The slow magic of a seed pushing a tiny sprout through soil defies the naked eye. A rose unfolds in its own time.

Likewise, the plan the Lord has for us doesn't unfold along our human timetable. When you rush ahead, when you wish for things to happen sooner, then

Continued on next page

> *Be patient, therefore, brethren, until the coming of the Lord. Behold, the farmer waits for the precious fruit of the earth, being patient over it until it receives the early and the late rain.*
>
> James 5:7

patience

you are attempting to alter God's divine plan. Let your daily life follow His schedule. Enjoy what you are facing right now, and rest in the knowledge that God knows the way.

Consider the story of the tortoise and the hare. The hare could run fast, and he believed his speed guaranteed his winning the race. The tortoise, on the other hand, knew the importance of keeping sight of his goal. He moved along at his own pace, never stopping, never doubting that he could win. And he did! Likewise, when we focus on the goal of living our lives according to God's plan, we will win by taking slow, steady steps every day—not by rushing and trying to run ahead.

Exercise patience: Practice staying cool; accept your present situation; celebrate being in the right place at the right time. Above all, do not give up, but rather to wait and endure until God's purpose is revealed.

patience

O God, I know the universe is unfolding according to Your plan, and yet I sometimes rush ahead impatiently. I believe that everything happens in its own time. Thank You for Your eternal patience with me, and forgive me when I fail to show the same forbearance to my brothers and sisters. Lead me to accept Your will and to wait patiently as it is revealed to me.

Temper

Men are like steel. When
they lose their temper,
they lose their worth.

Chuck Norris

*Nothing does reason more right, than the
coolness of those that offer it: For Truth often
suffers more by the heat of its defenders,
than from the arguments of its opposers.*

William Penn

*Many people lose their tempers merely
from seeing you keep yours.*

Frank Moore Colby

*When you're in the right, you can
afford to keep your temper. When in
the wrong, you can't afford to lose it.*

Anonymous

temper

If you've ever observed a stranger having a temper tantrum, you know how silly it looks. And worse than that, when we lose our temper, we are likely to say and do harmful things that we'll later regret.

Jesus set a great example for us when He was on Earth. No matter what the people around him did, he stayed calm. People cursed him, betrayed him, and in the end killed him—and yet he never responded to them in anger. When you feel yourself getting angry, take a time-out and get yourself back under control. You can take pride in following the model of Christ.

Everyone should be quick to listen, slow to speak and slow to become angry, for man's anger does not bring about the righteous life that God desires.

James 1:19-20

Refrain from anger, and forsake wrath! Fret not yourself; it tends only to evil.

James 1:9-10

temper

Heavenly Father, as I go
through the day, help me to
turn away from situations
that might lead to anger and
from people who are display-
ing anger. Remind me of the
love Jesus showed to His
oppressors, and let me follow
His guide wherever I go.

Parable: The Mustard Seed
Mark 4:30-32

And he said, "With what can we compare the kingdom of God, or what parable shall we use for it?

It is like a grain of mustard seed, which, when sown upon the ground, is the smallest of all the seeds on earth; yet when it is sown it grows up and becomes the greatest of all shrubs, and puts forth large branches, so that the birds of the air can make nests in its shade."

Repentance

Repentance is bringing one's conduct
up to the level of his ideals.

> Anonymous

Of all acts of man repentance
is the most divine. The
greatest of all faults is to
be conscious of none.

> Thomas Carlyle

Repentance is another name for aspiration.

> Henry Ward Beecher

The only vice that can not be forgiven
is hypocrisy. The repentance of a
hypocrite is itself hypocrisy.

> William Hazlitt

repentance

Some things in life are unavoidable, sin being one of them. We all fall short at one point or another, but the righteous thing to do is to acknowledge our sin.

Through acknowledging our wrongdoing we are able to feel regret and remorse. The act of repenting for our mistakes puts us into a state of humility, allowing us to receive the gratifying forgiveness that God has promised all of us.

Repentance, true repentance, will cleanse our heart and our mind of the negative energy caused our transgressions, bringing us closer to the warmth and comfort of the love of God.

Take heed to yourselves; if your brother sins, rebuke him, and if he repents, forgive him.

Luke 17:3

And Peter said to them, "Repent, and be baptized every one of you in the name of Jesus Christ for the forgiveness of your sins; and you shall receive the gift of the Holy Spirit.

Acts 2:38

Index

About the author

Christopher Armour is president of Armour&Armour Advertising. Before founding the full-service agency, he worked at *The Tennessean* in Nashville in a variety of positions including sportswriter. He is also the author of *The Wisdom of Fishing*.

Armour is a 1978 graduate of Yale University. His wife Jan is his partner in the firm.

For more information, contact
Foxglove Press
939 Camp Nakanawa Road
Crossville, TN 38571
1-877-205-1932